You Get What You Ask For

Shaaron Carswell Jackson

Shaaron Carswell Jackson

Copyright © 2024

All Rights Reserved

I personally Thank you!

Shaaron Carswell Jackson

Author

Congratulation, on purchasing my book. Today is the start of a better you because you have put yourself in the position to receive what I am sending and what you are going to do to get back: to faith. This book is a collection and you becoming the person you need to be now for greater you

"Holding"

What's been holding you back in life.

Now your faith will arrive back in place.

Let go, Let your greatness shine! Speak and Deliver

Now it time to attract your success through your faith and the way people look at you.

Map out

Map out from what use to do that stop you! And what you are going to start doing

Now remove that – above
map and work on the new
positive you. Be empowered,
and encourage that you are
not in your vehicle alone, the
driver starting the wheel
knows the route to take and if
their light at the of the tunnel

Dedication

Mary Louise Jackson

Thank God to my mother-in-law Mary Louise Jackson; I love you too!

Thank God, Miss Jackson, we were able to talk and laugh and share some excitement, and we kept it real; your son and your family are real with me, too, because of you. I tell them all that you lived during the hard times/when people had nothing but growing families, and they did not have the smarts, to become an entrepreneur, know or take on their own responsibilities, but they had a vision your knowledge, and I applaud you.

Mom, you must have had some real insight about Keith, and I you never shared it with me, but I understood my photo, drawn by my husband, was kept on the wall in your living room, they Keith's art teacher worked on a photo of me at Arts High School in north New Jersey in the classroom, I learned from you, Keith and he shared conversations about how Shaaron is doing sharing your concern about me and what business direction, I was going in and understood you were ready to partner with me, Wow we missed that, but I got your son, Keith, We love you, missing you.

Dorothea my Mom

This book is dedicated to the woman I love, my mother Dorothea; she has left behind a legacy of Adopting children, and for that, it will be passed on because they will spread the word of homecare or share in their off springs that made a difference in their life Dorothea made me believe if you don't who will she always says draw your blueprint and then put your higher superior in it to take you where you need to go, and that's how I live my life by his direction Dorothea I'll never go a day without a thought of you I will never forget the day at a Car dealership you stood and looked over a lot of vehicles you spoke of hope I am not getting a lady to leave this world because life was giving you what you had begun to as far or should I hope for I learned that recompensing on earth that when you get to heaven God wouldn't you out of this world with nothing you must get what you asked for down on earth.

You asked for me to have a family, and you wanted to see that before you left this world; you spoke to me, and that said in the event that I die, you will have sisters and brothers; you got just that you asked for, and I got the storms, that came with your wish, I thank God for what you ask for you had no you would get just what you asked for you would have put in words to God exactly what you wanted to leave for me.

I love you anyway, for you did all you knew to do to make

my life happy and not lonely.

Now returned back to sleep. I love you, and I am sorry to disturb you.

Acknowledgment

Thank you, honey, to my wonderful husband; keep the faith; continue to protect and provide love and worship with me and strengthen me as we show each other this is the manifestation of God's promise for us with equal glory.

To my husband, Keith Jackson, where do we go from here right to the top? I'm glad you love me, and you did what you did and had to do to keep yourself open for what you asked for in life; I'm sure you had no clue as to what you would get, but you held onto your faith, and your wish was granted by your side. Jesus Christ, your savior, I know him now; look back because you have said to me many times your mother had to know what was going to happen. Thanks for being a part of my life. It's beautiful when you get what you asked for; it was written that you were going to get what you asked for, but at the right time, not before; thanks for walking back into my life; it's a beautiful thing when you get what you asked for, faith believes in yourself restore your faith and finally using it to the occasion fade, when you change your way of thinking you change your way of doing, Keith’s Faith comes by way of hearing not seeing it's not there, Faith deals with you, your feelings and emotion.

You, the private you, the public you!

Contents

Preface

The book was written to lay down the truth about you, you asked for it, and it shall be done with faith; you believe and stand on faith; the chase drives you on your superior highway to write your story; remember the vehicle was driven because your blueprint is in action and any mistakes will be corrected as you progress because Jesus knows the way your superior pulls out his folder for your destiny and for every step you take he takes to the plant is there you.

Must follow and believe in faith and what can happen in moment poverty to success in a second calling, and you believe in his calling; my superior sets examples of loyalty and obedience to God; he remains faithful to his heavenly father and understands all types of circumstances despite all types of opposition suffering.

He remained faithful to his heavenly father under all types of circumstances and despite all types of opposition and suffering.

Jesus firmly and successfully resisted Satan's Temptations (Mathew 4:11-110)

AT ONE TIME, SOME OF JESUS OWN RELATIVES DID NOT PUT FAITH IN HIM, EVEN SAYING THAT HE

WAS OUT OF HIS MIND." (Marks 3:21)

Opening of the Book

You get what you asked for at the opening of the book

There is no substitute for what you believe in your faith, your strength, your commitment to your covenant of peace; you asked for it, and it is given by the king, or you're hirer superior.

God is doing great things in answering prayers, so it's time for you to start and wait for your prayers to be answered; this is faith; let this year be the best year of your life through faith and prayer. God is ready to help you recall your dreams and goals

Life is not a circus nor dress rehearsal, but you can be put down, laugh at talk about, and where is your faith life is no dress rehearsal; you have one life to think about, share, and do what you have to in order to live an abundant life if you don't put your faith and your attitude together you can't win you will be the best at whatever your goals are and your plans for the future and going through.

Have you ever heard of an elephant that will remain with its trunk down and never have concerned about what could happen to you if you just don't trust in your faith? You could have won the battle and arrived at the top of your game.

Think about your life and what you want out of it and why you should have faith, and why you should not have trusted. I am sure you will say, why not trust? Why not plant A seed and watch I grow? There's no reason why you should not start today trusting in yourself, and your faith will manifest itself.

Picture of God on the cross here

You get what you asked for by Shaaron Carswell Jackson

INRI
ith God all things are possible." St. Matthew 19:

Transformation Page Total Recall of Self

Looking at R from an educational point of you are has many meanings; it being the 18th letter in the lineup of the alphabet has given it virtually the most qualified position. Man is considered an adult in his 18th year was taking on many responsibilities such as being Reliable in one job and caring for one family and requiring restorations and total recall of all things one has learned from childhood; now, on a spiritual Side, one must be reborn therefore getting a new store one must replenish or give up Worley things and follow our Lord and Savior one must remove all sinful thoughts and activities one must require the love and respect that our Lord and Savior has given us in order to reap the fruits of our labor, and then one must be righteous and receive the gift of the Holy Ghost that which brings all things to our remembrance.

A nurse must stand in readiness to meet the needs of God's people; she has to be respected t the pastor and the church family, the nurse, must be teachable to endure sound doctrine; she has to be slow to anger and hold her tongue no matter what the circumstances and enjoy your hardiness as a good soldier in this army enclosing our clothes is the book in the New Testament revelations and divine truth God blesses you loving my mom. In remembrance of Mother’s spiritual faith meeting the needs of God's people, this was her own writings

We ask in Jesus name prayers for all.

Prayers for prosperity and guidance something are true! Yes, it may be true your family loves you!

That a matter of belief, matter of faith, your whole life is lived by faith whether you know, or the better weather understand it or not.

Faith can move mountains, and option

Be positive at all times, don't worry about past mistakes, and remember that there is nobody on this earth that hasn't made a mistake; not even the past is gone, but you right now, to live and enjoy.

Blessing of property, please deliver us from want. Help us to ease our struggles. Have faith in all you think of because when you think and believe in what you have thought and spoken about, positive results will follow.

It's keeping the faith

Prayer For All

(Prayer for prosperity @gudiance)

Dear heavenly father, as I pray, allow the person reading my book to focus on their life and some of the letdowns and how they have transformed for the better so they understand where i was headed with this book and then how the transformation turned into my faith my higher power and give us all strength to move forward with all projects and option available to us all today, let us have your guidance for you know of the way and your wisdom every hour. We ask in jesus name that you watch over us and help us as we strive to do our best. Father, your blessing of property, please deliver us from want and help us to ease our struggles.

Father, we know you will never for sake us!

Whatsoever ye shall ask in prayer, believing, ye shall receive."

Mathews 21:22

Foreword

First, I want to thank God for his love and blessings, my husband (Keith Jackson) and my family. My Faith, wow! I Could never let it go. I want to see what's in store for me next. I have never thought that I could not have; I'm just waiting to get what's mine, Next Issue. I asked my superior for wisdom long ago, and he put me right where I could get it. From a funeral director's wife, seeing and meeting people with different challenges in life, due to death in their families, to living abundantly, having and doing just about what I want to do and traveling to many different places.

Having "that faith" means that you can't stop believing what is about to happen to you because you've put it out to the universe. You are a star in your own rights because you are constantly thinking about what is going to take place or how you're going to make your next move. That's positive! That's what faith is all about! Things not seen but hoped for. Positive results that would put you where you need to be. I'm sure you've heard this saying, "Devil, get out of my way". He will step into your life from time to time, but you must dismiss him and move on with your plans to be successful. If you live long, you will Y de definitely stumble on blocks that are heavy and hard to move out of your way. But be strong and careful, and do what needs to be done to clear the removal.

Remember, God is sure! He fulfilled his promises throughout generations, and he continues to fulfill his covenant of peace. I wish all who read my story of faith may prosper and be in good health even as their soul prospers.

Behold I send the promise of my father upon you need Luke 24: 29

Let's get started writing today

Before I began let me share this with you I was preparing for my wedding and had spoken to my niece Candice on the phone to pick me up of course my second marriage we would go looking for a dress for my wedding she told me she would drop me off of course my second at the dress shop and would later pick me up for the store once she completed her errands well it didn't turn out like that the store was closed So I welled up going with her to Pathmark where they had on sale a computer lab I could not believe it because before I left home that morning I received a call about purchasing a computer but the price was out rages so I turned it down I had just said to myself a week ago the first thing that I would want to be doing with the money for my wedding was to purchase a laptop computer all I can say to myself once we got in the store was wow I couldn't believe what I had thought about is right near the sequence Valore the secrets Laura Candace said to me you want when I said yes I'll pay you later all I could do was think to myself I kept it to myself in the life of Christ seeing myself in this store in Montclair New Jersey that I would never thought I'd be going to get a computer I had asked for it and it came before time thing you see is the secret of law of attraction is well you get what you asked for it once you plant your seed walk away, my manuscript was first type by this computer.

Life is not a circus nor a dress rehearsal, but can be put down laugh at and left alone. Life is not a dress rehearsal, you have one life to think, share and do what you have to do in order to live in an abound life. If you don't put your faith in go and your attitude you will remain with your trunk down and never have a concerned about what could had happened for you if you just trusted in your faith and superior, you could have won and arrived at the top.

Think about your life and what you want out of it and why you should have faith and why you should not trust. I'm sure you will say why not trust, why not planned a see and watch it grow. There is no reason why you should not start today trusting in you and your faith will manifest itself.

Chapter One
Are You Here to Pick Me Up?

Start the vehicle let's ride

Hawaii

Is Your Faith Off Track?

Reach Your Higher Power

=

Change Your Filter and Be Transformed

God is the same today and yesterday. Remind yourself of who your God is, where is your faith, are you being tested by God. Remember what he has done for you!

Pray and fast for faith will arrive. You don't have to worry anymore.

Has your mountain shaken and you don't know which way to go?

God see where you are, act and he going to bring out your faith. Keep it on high.

Remember, winner never quit and loser never get started. Ask God and believe in what you ask for. Remember you're not the driver. You're the owner giving directions as to where you want to go from the backseat and God, your superior has his eye on you from the rear view mirror.

Overcome rejections, survive in down time.

God got a plan for you.

We all go through something sometime but you have what it takes. Hope, pray and you will receive what God has for you. Be encouraged, for the Lord hears and sees you asking for this change.

Just continue to fill his purpose!

Joy come when in the morning.

Believe, grace forgive all sins.

God made a promise to Joshua and when you keep your focus in God, you shall have perfect peace.

Remember, you are nothing without superior because when you're weak, your superior is stronger. Turn it over to him.

Imagine This is Life

You Want to Create and Get Busy with Your Faith, Then Will Arrive Your Greatness in Time

Imagine what your faith can bring you. From your growing years to your youth.

She is clear superstar and making the charts she has song with and continuous to sing with Mega celebrities, she was first introduced as Miss Fashion Queen (1981) Faith Renee Evans

Came from New Jersey was chosen Queen in my founding pageant by Shaaron C Jackson, Faith is now the Big Hip-Hop Soulful singer. The first lady of Bad Boys record entertainment by Shawn Puffy Combs. Now Sean John, has exceeded some of the world well know designers in Europe.

Getting what you hope for and ask for.

Climbing to the next level of faith – Didn't do it any other way!

Getting what I dream of and hope for a SURPRISE 21st BIRTHDAY

PARTY AGAIN WHAT I DREAMED ABOUT BEING IN A

BEAUTY PAGEANT

Getting what you ask for.

A chance to be among pageant contestant

"I will instruct thee and teach thee in the way which thou shall go"

Psalm 32.8

Irvington girl among finalists in Miss N.J. Teenager Pageant

SHAARON CARSWELL

Keep your faith on at all times. The Driver knows when and where to drop you off!

Chapter Two
Faith Is A Blessing For Opportunity

There is nothing that holds us back from our higher powers.

Be free today then it will happen!

Faith

What is faith? Is it waiting? Is it Believing? Is it coming or is it tomorrow. No, faith is now! Right Now! But you're right! But you're right!

But you have to believe that it's gonna

Happen that way, yes that way

The way it is supposed to happen.

Faith is good times; faith is your choice. Faith happen each day. We all have something we want and wish for so dearly. We are trusting and believing that it will happen the way we thought of.

You can only align your thoughts as how you think it will happen and then let time move your thoughts to manifestation, faith is blessing for opportunity.

"*You can get what you*

ask for" **Even**

Hawaii

I have everlasting faith.

Everlasting faith, prosperity and guidance is this what you want – Let your higher power and it will be done!

My faith took me to Hawaii. After a phone call I received, I was told to pack my bags, we are going to Hawaii. I put it on my faith burner and it was deliver delivered by the driver in the front seat. ☺

Where are you going?

When two people face the same issue or concern, one may become depressed and feel they don't know which way to turn while the person with faith draws closer to God or their higher power. Because they know he will bring them out. God will never leave you or forsake you so hold on to your dreams.

Because change will come in the morning.

Sometimes in life you will have difficult times but having faith after you look back, you see they were really a blessing Sometimes you get up, sometimes you are tested by the superior. *Corinthians 10;13*

Jesus said, "I came that they (you and I all Christians) Might have life and might have it abundantly" (John 10:10)

If you have no faith and think average, than that's what you will get you may think there is certainly nothing abundant about life.

If you faithfully yield to the will of God and surrender you way and allow your faith to be first and believe.

Faith Helps

You get what you asked for! When we plant a seed and water it, we expect a miracle to happen. There are no preconceptions these days as to what miracle can happen for the seed to grow and if it doesn't come up, we are ready to take that pack of seed back to the hardware store and say something wrong, like those seeds didn't come up.

It's our faith that we believe that the seed should start to come up, and it is our faith to believe we will have just what we purchased. Tomato, cucumber, whatever you have planted in this life.

So now you know what opportunities faith can present and what your expectations are. Now use your faith to manifest and bring your glory begin to have the life you have dreamed of and let others watch and wonder how you are doing what you are doing.
You get what you asked for.

"*He leadeth me in the path of righteousness*"

Psalm 23.3

Getting what I ask for a trip to Paris, having fun, loving my passion and exploring.

Giving Thanks to Your Higher Power

Faith has truly brought an inspiration in my life. I could always remember my mother saying to me, you have faith and you rely on it.

My mom would always say to me I have faith in you. This is truly what has and continue to keep me on the fast track of life because we face challenges. So, I chose the faith and journey I find to be the most comforting and God's best plan for me! This is my truth,

I know there is nothing that the Lord and I can't accomplish, it might just take some time, but that with everyone. We all have a journey, some arrive early and can't believe they are there, and don't know that they are there or have arrived!

People always say that thank God, the Good will always outweigh the bad. With faith you know more good times are on the way.

Thanks to faith, I keep my plate full and never let no one unbalance my thought process. I know you get what you ask for.
I've seen in manifestation, to glorification.

Are you ready to receive what you have asked for?

Get ready, it could be dropped off in your lap and you won't be able to receive or will you!

Chapter Three
Value Your Faith and Teachings 365 Days A Year

Faith

Believe with all your heart that good things will happen for your than that's what you will receive the best.

If you are thankful, giving and forgiving – you are said to be full of faith and faith brings about things store for, comfort and cheer. All around the world, peace love and understandings.

When you are able to reach out to those whom have hit Rk bottom and share your faith people enjoy that for the moment and began to see that there is light at the END of the TUNNEL. On the other side and wake up and in some cases these faith is RENEW and it began to move in positive direction and thins are then Hope for again but if you never let your faith leave you – things Hope for will soon be seen.

Value your faith and teachings 365 days per year. Each on your another day check to what probability are going to be taking place because your faith is increasing for manifestation. I reach out and spoke to young women and ask her about her faith she researched her definition before she told me about her faith.

No matter what I ask about faith it remain the some to some

it all up, it all about a higher being , then self. But it's if you believe, some did and some don't, but do you believe.

Mercedes wright the young ladies el reach out to about her faith went on to pay that with the money fare of faith it has confused her and her faith is not wear it should be, Question is where should your faith be.

I went back to her and question her on how can you get your faith back to wear it need to be,

She pen it up with love trust and believe.

Take a look at the conversation she shared and wrote for me.

What is Faith?

Faith in general the persuasion of the mind that a certain statement is true, belief in & assent to the truth of what is declared by another, based on his or her supposed authority, and truthfulness.

Faith is the confident belief or trust in the truth or trustworthiness of a person, concept or thing. – Wikipedia's Definition.

What is Faith To Me?

Asking me the question do you have faith so broad and unliteral, faith has so many meanings to so many different people; but my faith I believe and have faith in what is seen and proven rather than, heard and unjustified. When I think of the word faith the first entity that comes to my mind when I always heard the word faith was God, the father. To have faith in him at the most high. My faith in God hasn't been as strong as it should only because what is written, I am told to believe. So many different religions, so many different ways but when it's all said and done, 1 God we pray to, 1 God we call on, 1 God we have faith in, because it was given to us through these multiple books to believe that God has created this world that man so obviously proclaimed. There is only one God in my opinion, No religion He is amongst us all, No matter his name; God, Jesus, Allah, Buddha , Jehovah; and all. His many other faces through cultural, have faith in God.

So, ask me again about my faith… Faith is what faith does. To have faith in myself, that I will succeed, I will humble myself, I will come to pass with and have faith in that this world we're living will one day become a much better and deserving place to bare.

To have faith to me, only means to have goals a mere substitute for trust or belief. We take this word Faith and try an take apart the meaning, but it means nothing more than trust as simple as the one lable word that it is, as simple as Love or Lust which typically people automatically fall victim to what I call trust genocide. Love and Faith concurs nothing but destruction eventually with or without faith, so to me faith.... trust… belief… has only one natural meaning…

You can only trust to have faith and believe that whatever it is that you have faith in is and will ultimately be faithful.

What You Expect Shall Happen Having Faith.

Having your faith for Better Day, name that angel that has faith and celebrate her faith with other by offering them experience they would have never been able to do or afford or run thought of.

Her name is Oprah Whitfrey she will go down in glory leaving a legacy to be carry on.

She as television host is able to reach massive of people and pay forward to them, those have reach rock bottom and some that just needed a handshake she given many glory and honor they deserve.

She has encourage other reach out to those's that are in need, those without faith in some case to see that there is light at the end of the tunnel.

Their Faith was in some case were lost and renew when she impact their life.

Remember, if you never let your faith leave those things hope for will soon be seen. Oprah has said on National Television how she feels when she giving image, the moment. So pray what you perceive you will possess.

Control Your Journey, Health, Wealth , Exercise

Reduce stress with looting pistachio

Eating Salmon and exercising – not every day but when you feel the stress level high.

The higher power that your truly believe in write open your heart and allow you to Roz on high gear understand that you will have beliefs and this will help you to notice your faith and it existence.

We all have it you are powerful don't give your power to the unknown. Believe that your higher power will produce. Surrounding yourself with position people will help you continue faith and leave those alone that hinder your faith and progress.

Develop relationship with people who share some values as you. Make a change, shake off your doubts and then go for it.

Check out your options and act find or approach to the future and turn today's dream into fact, start on the course of your chance, look at what life has to offer, listen to your inner self.

Nothing and nobody can come before prayer, God the holy spirit and his son allowed us to come together, think, observe, bring forth our talents that once were unforeseen into existence, there is nothing that you can't do – there is nothing that you can't dream, there is no where you don't go as along as you are trying and not just waiting to fail or allow other to come into your thought and redirect you. You can have it all for certain of what we do not see but believe ones hope for will open your faith down into existence.

Believe

To believe is to know in you heart that life is happening exactly as it meant to happen for you and things hope for are on their way to you, and that you have done.

What must be carry out for it to happen this is your faith start up the ignition now.

Miracles

Once the seed is planted watch the bloosm you will be astounded as what will happen.

We become surprise and amazed at what we have started.

Imagine

Whatever you hope for come in to reach when you imagine what is it you want?

Now see yourself in it.

Care

Treasure the time spent. Share your with other and give them direct on how to move forward on their hope of faith you are not alone in any moment.

Love

Have faith that the ones you think love you do. Because it nothing their but air and conversation that said it love in the all in all it’s nothing but faith that you believe this person love you.

Chapter Four
Creating your vision through faith works

Sharon engaging with different events

My success or getting what you ask for! As your dream of entrepreneur

Running Beauty Pageant and Promoting

Becoming an Entrepreneur

All Things What So Ever Ye Shall Ask, Believing Ye Shall Receive

– Matthews 21:22

What do you want because you get what you ask for!

You see you get what you ask for but you must be on the same page as your higher power and it will be delivered. But are you willing to wait, are you willing to go the extra mile. You may have to work or go through storm to receive it.

Even business professional goes through storms to achieve their goals. Robert Kiyosaki sold 26 million copies of Rich Dad Poor Dad but he try to go the traditional route but nobody wanted his manuscript. So he did it himself and marketed his book – that been on NewYork times best sellers list several times. But what did he have? I call it faith. What you need to get to the top of YOUR DREAMS. We all have Dreams and Wishes but you must learn to work your Faith to get you what you want. We are all powerful – don't desire your power to unknown believe. When your higher power will produce my higher power being God. Only two way to get it, what you want, is to plan it, seek it and vision it "creating your faith through Faith works"

Let's list some goals for next 5 years and create a vision brand.

Goal Create A Vision Board

What you dreamed of = what will manifest it self.

Have fun and watch your faith = achieve.

Understand where your are going watch how you move forward on your vision board.

So let began by filling out our needs, to do in the next five years goal plan.

Use magazine and article to highlight your projections.

You will need photos to show your passion for what it is, that you want and for your faith, continue faith, to continue it's journey for the thing your certain of what you do not see.

Let's get started on ideas and now, your unlimited mind set as to where you want to go in your life. No limits please.

Put your picture and photographs and place on your refrigerator as your canvas, it's the best, you see it daily as a constant reminder.

Knowledge alone is not enough, though for without faith it is impossible to please (GOD) will Hebrews 11:16

So it's important that you not take your faith lightly. Learn to be strong and hold on to what you truly think will happen and your superior will do the rest you must give him a day.

You Get What You Ask for Use Your Mind, Your Faith and You Will get What You Ask For.

I never forgot on television a women appear and she spoke about the mind and how it can take you where you need to go it just a matter of speaking and think and believing that you will receive for what you are certain of because of your faith manifestation that just what I did when I heard this woman speak I decide that I was going to Paris I believe and I saw myself their and before you know it I was boarding a plane to Paris.

Before I knew it my goal was accomplished and their I was on Chants Deleyese and visiting the Eiffel Tower my faith got me there.

I believe in what I wanted then working towards – what would be needed to get me there.

This woman that appeared on television Programme was Maya Angela, found out many years later.

Posture, Good Attitude and progression – Right thinking, right thinking, right action, right reaction.

How do you know if your faith is working is to actually see it working?

So start seeing and watching and believing your life reflect all the things we say.

Watch you faith.

Jesus Christ showed in a powerful way through his own manner of response, the vital importance of right reaction to ever circumstances of life. Confronted by the negative attitudes of the Pharisees and other religious leaders, he persistently moved forward in having faith in God.

Jesus had faith in God all the while he was the focus faultfinding. He criticized because of the way he ministered to the seekers of healing because, he sat down to eat with the tax collectors and the sinners (Luke 5:30) and because the diciples, on the Sabbath plucked and ate some grain. LK 6:11 as a result of Jesus faith the paralyzed man by , letdown through the roof by his friends rose beforethem... went home glorifying God (LK 5:25)

Kept right on doing God's work.

Jesus Maintained self control never trying to harm his opposers. (1 peter 2:21-23)

Life is a gift from God (Psalm 36:9)

So remember to pray to our father in the heavens Matthews (6:9)

" no matter what it is that we ask according to his will he hears us" (1 john 5:14) so we may pray for anything that in harmony with God's will ask for help to do the right by God.

Ask for guidance in making wise decision, and for strength in coping with difficulties (Jame 1;5)

Back in 1985, I decided that was going to get married, so that's exactly what I did, A Cathedral Bride my parents so happy for myself, my husband and I blew it out with 265 guests attendance. The wedding was held at the first Baptist church in small town, lall seashell new jersey.

We had two pesters that officiated the wedding. We had a blast and took a two weeks' vacation in Florida Keys to the end of route 95. He took my pictures. At the sign of 95, next stop, A Acapulco, New Mexico where my dream hotel came full circle.

A Acapulco Princess a dream a thought this become real. Did I get what I ask, for you bet!

I had no idea when – how – I would arrive but I knew it would manifest itself because I feel strange about my faith and my trust turn over to him.

You see this was all I created in my mind that I was going there by my creator had to put it all together for it to work let me share just how my journey began when I walk in to a funeral parlor due to death and I saw the pictures of this man I said that I was going to marry him not knowing his situation. I knew that I was going to be his wife and it would work out just like that, can't help to tell you the truth but I got just what I ask for!

My husband and I began our life it was great! We shared my magical moment together.

I remember my husband saying to myself when we purchase a house that would be the last house he wants or purchase, well he got first what he asked for and I sad that would not be the last one I am purchasing.

Faith Was Taught By Our Parents At Early Age

"Faith was taught by our parents at a young age" For example, your parents would say to you – you can do it! Just try – they had faith in you and encouraged you that you could do it, and they would be right beside you if you encountered any problem if you didn't make it; they say just keep your head up; you'll make it the next time. And you succeeded in that until next time, and when you were ready, your faith was at a new all-time high because you were now ready to remove all training wheels and make a go at whatever it was you were trying to prove or do, so release and believe in your faith it will take you where you want to go, Right Now!

Get your mind on your Harvest, and must you promise conversant.

Chapter Five
Manifestation Comes Glory

Therefore I say unto you, take no thoughts for your life. What ye shall eat or what ye shall nor yet for your body what ye shall put on.

-Matthews 5:21

Things That I Asked for and Received

Your attitude and your faith will take you places and give you a more abundant life longer, and you will be more suitable and be around much longer. Life's not perfect, but the ingredients which you use to be persistent and perseverant in your life will make the difference for it to be fruitful.

I will never forget the first time I visited the Bahamas, I was taken in a room for time sharing introduce to myself and others. Time-sharing, this was amazing to get-your-heart all-inclusive and breathtaking wanting you to go to the hotel for breathtaking ground at the Acapulco Princess in Acapulco Mexico- my faith took over, and I said to myself I am going there- my faith was put on notice let's begin to shift our thoughts and faith to be put on notice your faith and receiving what will be owed to me by my coveient of peace promised by driver off my vehicle it happened, and it can happen to you too.

Allow your much higher power to take you where you need to go!

Faith is waiting on you to let it go and allow it work to manifest it happen for me. And you are just a thought away; don't you deserve to get what is waiting for you?

Now let's increase our value with the thought we want and people that work the same for you and the good we want for ourselves.

Getting what I Ask For My Day and Dream to Go to Acapulco.

It may be a goal of yours, a dream, or an imaginative thought; put it into place with faith because it can be achieved and put into place where your faith is.

You Get What You Ask for….

I'm being asked to tell this story so that others may want to be a part of what faith can do for you and you're thought process and how it can keep you on a positive track in life. The only spirit that knows your direction and what the outcome will be before you. His name is Jesus, and for those non-believers, it is a higher calling. Only they know what is on the plate you eat! Your thought process is the success of your life moving forward; of course, we don't know everything, so there will be mistakes made; that's called learning, but having a higher calling makes your load easier. Seek His Kingdom first, and the choice is yours…

Knowing you're a child of the highest high makes you victorious many confirmations for me to have a crime to pass such as having a queen name, Victoria (one of the cheetah girls Kell from Disney sisters of Newark, New Jersey) and Faith Evans, Newark, New Jersey.

God will give you greater all the time! Did the subprime house foreclosure put you back on the burner,

and didn't you think you were the only person out there that was concerned in the world?
The economic crisis was happening to us all… but with your faith, it could have been an eye-opener for you.

I am sending you another western union; make sure you get what I'm sending you, and you break it down and let manifestation take place to bring you glory.

I want to share with you that one day I was heading out to lunch from my 9 to 5 pm job and got with a co-worker Simine Corter; we decided that we would be going to Roy Rogere for a burger at a just food chain, we enjoy a great lunch, and I told her to let's go over to the Mercedes dealership after lunch that was just across the street from where we were having lunch. She agreed but thought I was crazy; no, I wasn't crazy. I had chosen and was just waiting for manifestation; it was just a timing situation that would have to take place before I would be dreaming a Mercedes.

One day I was leaving home in my car, and I spoke to my higher Superior, and I said, I want a new Mercedes, he spoke to me and said when you pay off your present vehicle, I will put you into a new Mercedes and he did just that I got my brand new emerald green Mercedes.

When you change your way of thinking, you change your way of doing; faith comes by way of having, not by seeing it not there.

It's how God or your superior activates your Faith Wants.

Here is another dream I had and how my faith allowed me to focus on what was about to happen, let me tell you. One day I was thinking at my desk that I was going to go looking for my New Cadillac Car, you see I have always loved things that had value. If I must say to myself, I had a dream the night before that showed me the color of the car would be Ivory Blue and White.

I walked the lot of the dealership back and forth and still hadn't found the vehicle I liked; then I went into the showroom, and there was the vehicle on the showroom floor, I saw was my dream, and you get what you asked for, and this was it I told my salesperson to work up that order I had no cash, but three days I was on the road with my new car. I had all the elements for manifestation, the thought of the dream, the vision – and allowed for glory to be put in the mind and brought to life. Be careful you just might get what you ask for. Life is great, and God is good.

The faith you see is the only what is and what isn't, and it's not your call; it's your thought; it's someone higher than you and I that makes the total call; let it happen for you and to you.

Have you ever been in a situation? where the other person makes the call of what is to happen right now, or if the call is not followed through or what is what's going to happen or what could happen? And at that point, you make a decision, and you say if it's for me, then it will happen.

That's faith. You believe just what you are saying and believe this will happen for you.

Faith is now. You are taking a stand and believing what happens will be. God's will and only the best will happen for you. This is what is meant to be, but you must have the courage to believe this is what is meant to be because you have faith and believe in your faith and believe the outcome will be in your best interest. This is faith, only what is and what isn't. this book is for you and you. Speaking to everyone about creating and moving forward, you must have faith in everything you do. In order to make your actions come to pass, you must stop and think and have faith that the outcome will be green.

You Get What You Ask For

What you can hear can change your life! Just trust in God!

What you hear inside, hear the voice speaking to you.

If you have no faith = you will remain where you are and go no further until it happens to you.

Nothing thought of nothing done

Nothing will happen Except for what you – walk into!

I trust in our Lord and Savior and continue to do so, and I take life for what's attainable for me, dreaming and going on in the direction that God will have me go. There's no stopping me at no time. I continue to prepare different meals that I know my Father would want me to have and continue to wait and trust in His Holy name. I thank God I have led to you once again. Continue to build the city and the people God leads to you. And Lady J., we know the road has not been easy with all the members, but it will come to pass. Remember one thing; it takes a strong woman to stand behind a good man. Loving my family and church for good.

"Train Your Heart to Believe"

Give like God gave have a spirit of "faith." All the time, not just in bad times, but at all times. Listen to what is being said inside, that your Superior is speaking to you!

What is wanted! It can be achieved!

What is being said? Will give you directions!

My Pastor's Sermon – "Your thought Process"

Your change is a thought away, letting faith be in charge. Take and drop your thought off to Jesus and move on. Pastor Jefferson of Metropolitan Baptist Church, at 149 Springfield Avenue, Newark, New Jersey, spoke about your thought, your faith, and how it affects one. I thought to myself as the sermon began, this is what I'm talking about in my book about faith and that I needed to speak to him about my book. You get what you ask for. I was putting it together, and my thought process was about my book tour and signing and how wonderful it would be to have the signing right here at the church.

And I thought about how I could not forget about Pastor Jefferson because he has been an inspiration in his teachings to me. God has to lead me to address him in my book and has to lead me,
Shaaron, to his pasture of flock as if one of his sheep. Faith is what it takes to move forward in this life, and there is no other way. I'm praying that millions will read my book and be led to you, Pastor Jefferson.

A positive one, my motto is: You lose some of the time you go after, but you lose all the time you don't go after. You speak your thoughts into existence all the time. But you must speak all of what you want for it to happen. Example: It's like writing, and you begin to write, but you don't complete what you're writing. How will the reader be able to understand or translate what you are projecting unless he can read the whole situation that you have completed? Life is about destiny and faith.

Believing that you will get to where you need to be and your season. If it's your season now, where are you going? Sometimes you will have to let go in order to grow. That's what birds do. They let go of their young in order for them to grow. They have faith that they have prepared the young to fly on their own. So I say, "have faith and believe that you can and will be received by the masters that will do wonders with your thoughts and put them where they need to be."

KFC
Colonel's
SCHOLARS
Value up to $20,000 Over 4 Years
Sharonda Drew
Bogota, NJ
Kean University

Debra Robinson Spann is a friend of mine. I don't know her impact on her family but I she has had impact on my life and family and I thanks her.

I wasn't sure, as always, about the impact of the Glory and

the manifestation that has taken place in my life.

You get what you ask for, love too! I'm getting married and would like to have a reception after returning back from my honeymoon my girlfriend Debra called me but I had to stop a min I was thinking of having a reception at a fabulous place Pantagious for the bride to be, a beautiful place, that gives you awareness of being a bride, anyway Debra and I on the phone and said she would not be attending my wedding in Los Vegas, but she would like to give me a reception and that was sweet. My thought were put out to the universe law of attraction, I got what I asked for.

New cars that come to Puss

"You Get What You

Ask for" Just Wait and

See!

Chapter Six
Celebrity Status

Jesus said unto him, if thou cast believe, all things are possible to that belief. – Mark 9:23

Martin Luther King – 1929 – 1968

Born in Atlanta, Georgia.

Faith was!

I say almost all his life married to Correctia Scott and Children.

1955 life fired up when Rosa Parks refused to give her seat on the bus. Martin joined in for a segregation for busing the storm hit when his house was fire bomb. He was ready to face whatever would happen.

But he kept his faith.

Barack Obama told the people the struggle was real, but yes, we can; Martin wanted freedom and justice for all. You never know the storm you may have to go through to achieve your thoughts and what faith holds for you.

But you get what you ask for; claim it. It's yours; remember, when you are going through a tough time, you need to stay true to yourself and do what you believe in. You will always get lots of opinions, but perseverance is the key that will help you to reach greatness; your key to success is your belief; you believe, and faith will take you where you need to go, but it is not on our time it on someone higher than self.

Oh yes, if true! But what you have to go through to achieve what you hope for, have faith for believing it may be a storm for you to self. What you ask you look at the Bible, you will note a storm that had to take place departing the Red sea, Noah Art, but in these instead, God said he wanted to know where the faith was he gave the command to release that we all look for!

Martin Luther King Got What He Ask for

You see, you get what you ask for, but there may be storm, or, disappointment; only your higher power knows what will happen and when it will happen and to whom it will happen too!

Martin Luther King had a dream, he had faith and hope that one day we would all be able to rise to the occasion, and he got first what he asked for.

He was a Nobel prize winner, but his number one, in 1983, Ronald Regan signed and passed the Jan 3 Holiday bill became Martin Luther King day to celebrate the true meaning of what Martin Luther King stood for.

In his death, he is a legend and "he got what he asked for."

On this day, we celebrate the man who loved to ream A BIG

DREAM "to get what he asked for."

She is a clear superstar and making the charts she has sung with and continues to sing with mega celebrities that she was first introduced as miss Fashion Teen Queen 1981 Faith Renee Evans came from New Jersey was chosen queen in my pageant and founded by myself shown Shaaron C Jackson, she is now the big Hip-Hop soulful singer. The first face of Bad Boy Records entertainment by Shawn Puffy Combs, now Sean John, has exceeded some of the well-known designers in Europe.

Part of the secret to life is standing on your firm blueprint and commitment to believing with an equal key to faith.

I hear people all the time talking about these times; you must operate off faith.

My suggestion to all who think today is always you must keep faith at the same level all the time, not just any day, all day; it must be 360 degrees full circle no matter what the circumstances press on. Pray, pray will change things, and each time will pray for it, whatever it may be.

Faith and change are different. Faith is what happens, and change is what has to happen; let me say that again. Faith is what happens, and change is what has happened.

Michelle Obama

Michelle Obama, the first African American first lady, our new Etiquette of Power model, grace, confidence and intelligence adds up to true Rodiner Calvin Klein. Did she get what she ask for to become the first African American historic icon first lady as per Kate Betlo author she put it out that " projecting yourself in the world with fashion before answering at your call is magical faith and it appear the first lady did first that and now she empowered women of many ethnicities and creed with her elegance and fantastic choice in fashion remember to have faith and watch your appearance because your faith may take you where you want to go and you want to arrive in good taste and style, like our first lady and I haven't got the opportunity to ask her did she get what she wanted but I do no she step out on faith and applied herself and stood by her husband our first African historic President Barack Obama and the both love and continue to show and reflect value to African American family and what a difference they made as part of the American people that love and express life those opportunity for other in the fulfillment of this country and President Barack Obama continue to getting American people what we ask for in sharing opportunity with all to make for Great US of America.

Barack Obama

Barack Obama said yes, we can, and we did in numbers; they got out to vote, and everything happened just the way Barack thought it would happen.

Ask him I'm certain! He tells you it did!

His Inauguration will never be forgotten; the 44th American president of the United States and a Noble President that has been voted is to watch over us. It is a big challenge for a man that gets what he asks for because he believes in what he says and thinks; he believes in the time has come for us all to have to do what's for us. And to make a positive step in the direction of a better life for a continued great journey to the American dream for all.

Barack Obama said we have to work harder to uphold the idea that we all equally deserve the chance to pursue our own happiness.

Seek Peace and Dignity; yes, you can have what you ask for, Barack Obama wanted to be the President, and he got just what he asked for. Yes, we can, and you can get what you ask for.

Oprah Studio

Yes, that Oprah Studio, Chicago – I was there. That's right, I will never forget wanting to go to Oprah's show, but I asked for it, and I got just what I asked for.

I never forget overnight sitting home and receiving a call from a girlfriend of mine, and she said these exact words. I think it is getting ready to happen. I said that going to the pitch showcase in Chicago, she was excited she had just met Gayle King, and she stopped her and told her how unsuccessful she had been trying to get on the Oprah show.

Gayle King being positive and representations Oprah spirit said Joann to contact me with the information she provides, and she would respond and put her where she needed to be to get on the Oprah show.

The ticket Gayle King was able to get for us was fabulous with ground-breaking celebrities such as Micheal Jordan, Steve Wonders, top model Naomi Campbell, Iman Bowie and a makeover of severel different people. I got just what I hoped for in a fashion show, and that made my short vacation even brighter; you get what you ask for at his time. I'm part of the angels network, Thank God!

Michael Jackson

Michael Jackson – Top Billboard album charts told all his fans in London, "This is it" King of pop.

Michael Joseph Jackson: August (29, 1958 – June 25, 2009)

Wise is an American recording artist, dancer, singer, songwriter, musician and Philanthropist.

Conveys emotion in all the songs; he had charisma, talent unlimited Phenomenal talent; he loves to create for the audience and show experiences you will never forget; he was and remains an unbeatable icon that will live in the minds of lives forever, but Michael said something that this is it, A win and he would never perform again in London. Michael got what he asks for? From getting bullied to becoming the King of pop. Think about it! Why did he never perform again in London and time it up and tell the world this is it? Did he know? This would be it!

Christopher George Latore Wallace

May 1972, March 1997, known as Biggie Small was raised in Brooklyn, Deal Drugs, at an early age, got what he asked for, ready to die, but they brought him back to life on the big screen. Biggie always talked about the way he used to live and how he lives gave the exportation of a black life he use to sip champagne on his Birthday it was all dream and a life before his death, and then he told the world he was ready to die.

Did he get what he asked for?

From his expertation of gangster and his gender, this was to happen; Biggie made millions, the same as author Richard Wright who wrote the Native Sun about our society at another level.

Tupac Shakur

Tupac Shakur – June 16, 1971, to Sept 1996, known as 2 Pac sold over 75 million albums worldwide, making him one of the bestselling music artists in the world; Rolling Stone magazine named him 86th greatest artist of all time the last album he drop was named break it down the don Illuminati he got just what he told us to break it down.

Believe

To believe is to know in your heart that life is happening exactly as it is meant to happen for you and things hope for are on their way to you and that you have done what must be way out for it to happen (this is your faith start-up ignition)

It may take a moment to savor the quiet time. Miracles, it's all in time. We are unaware of what miracle could blossom once the seed is planted, and we are surprised and amazed at what we started.

Be inspired – by real people that love you!

Imagine

Whatever you hope for comes in to reach that was only the floor plan that you imagined would happen now is all there for you, the breath of air to release.

Care - Treasure the time

Spend their time with others and give them direction as to how to move forward on their hope of faith; you are not alone at any moment.

Chapter Seven
"Enjoying the Ride"

It's great to look back and not have the funeral Procession following you behind the limousine that your superior drives! Or what type of hat or crown is the driver wearing?

This assures of the time your about have!

Whatsoever ye Shall ask in prayer, believing, ye shall receive.

Matthew 21.22

God only responds to faith; conquer fear with faith; your actions to faith affect you!

Creative power inside of you! That effect on our life takes context and creates a simple approach to your testing through you.

Your level where you are performing turns your light up or down; if we have only what we have experienced, we have nothing, but if we have an inspiration of God. The vision is that we have more than we can experience; you have to know where you are, and you see the uncertainty and hope, for nothing are impossible with God.

Exodus 19.5.6

Now therefore, if you will indeed obey my force and keep my covenant, then you shall be a special treasure to me above all people, for all the earth is mine.

And you shall be o me a kingdom of priests and a holy nation; these are the words which you shall speak to the children of clorace.

It's important to know also the people you spend the most time with greatly impact your life. They shape your beliefs and value.

This could be your second chance to Ride!

You see, God even got a second chance to protect the world, and he kept his Faith; he knew that he had to save the world because people were treating each other so badly, so the father decided what to do. He figured out that he needed a son so man would have a second chance and his son would die for our sins. The sin of the people and thank god for his faith, his son was born and died again and was racing to love the world from our deadly sin and order to get to father you to return to the son. To have faith and believe, we all have choices and thoughts, and your faith could love the world from the problem; you may be the solution; we all have purpose and intention. Don’t throw you're away; your source could be overflowing that could help us love this world; your faith is your vision, product or service could be what we are waiting or your greatness could be what we love been waiting to present itself, but you must have belief in you, you may want what the wisdom of opportunity you could be the next Steve Jobs of Apple or the next Warren Buffet they see have forth in what they do and their superior knows their purpose in this life, they are just seeing it threw.

Be glad and rejoice for the Lord will do great things for you; never give up; believe you can win with faith!

Believe In the American Dream with Faith. Have You Enjoyed My Ride This Far?

“Now Where Your Faith”

“Keep it on, stay street your Faith.”

“Don’t Tell the driver to turn.”

Come on, let's take this ride together on the better side of life.

Relax; it doesn’t get better than this. Let God or your superiors do their job, and you do have faith.

There is nobody greater than you and your thoughts, so

make……

Now! If you know who’s driving the vehicle, can you let your faith take you where you need to or do you what to be in charge of everything? Let go and let God show up when you least expect it.

It’s proven you need help to build your empire. You need the right people to do their job to make the empire go up.

It's true someone is fond of you. So which way are you going to go now, and which way are you gonna let your mind go so that you can continue to grow your faith and get back on track at God's convenience?

How can you lead if you don't know how to lead – it's like going to college, getting your education and then getting the job of a lifetime. Only because you believe that was supposed to happen was what you have to do to get there. It was your belief that led you in that direction.

What I Seen on the View!

And manifestation started then

Acapulco Princess

It came true

Hey ladies, you know what I mean!

Chapter Eight
Now You See Who's Behind The Wheels Write your story on how you got your faith back on track

"I will never leave there."
Hebrews 13.5

God Had Faith

God had a purpose and a plan and had faith two! – For his resurrection.

He told them I must go to Jerusalem and suffer many things be killed and on the 3rd day. Be raised to life, and it happened, but he had what?

Faith and it happen

"it can happen for you to"

Your prediction

"Be strong and of good courage." Joshua 1:9

Faith In Yourself

Have faith in God, encourage yourself, envision victory, you have the power to win at your choice, using your power your thought you how the victory to master any suggestion, you put on your mind you have the power to envision, think and do what you envision, learn to listen to you and act an only the positive thought you have in your mind, you will let yourself free and allow your resource to take you higher faith to your choice of trust in your God.

Remember, "you get what you ask for," one idea followed by the action of you believe that trust and hold on to ensure your faith manifestation will be revealed.

1. Here's your recipe to getting back on track with your faith forwardness to the property with your higher power; remember:
2. Faith gives people purpose; find yourself when you have no faith, you become oppressed, frustrated, and don't know what will happen, but with faith, you see yourself!
3. You must put yourself in a positive state of mind; nothing will happen that you and your higher power can't get through any day; all will come to pass.
4. You deserve to have the best in your life. See yourself as a role model and person; look go to your for good choice and best option, have well thought now to free yourself and let God be in charge.
5. Are you in Health Environment? Your surrounding, can you make a good choice for yourself? Affect how you think and your thought process.
6. You have support. (Handy friend that empowers you to be the best) encourage you, practice meditation to let go and let it work for you.

7. Are you ready to make a decision for yourself? Meaning are you willing to let go and let God?
8. Transition and transform to receive what your God has in store for you. He has and continues to fulfill his commitment to peace. For each and everyone, you have to let your God
   do his work, and you take your concern and thoughts and leave them to ve competed.
9. Let faith ride to victory with equal manifestation-so you can have glory and you can move forward because you have no God or the best on the way you plan and what you expect will happen.
10. Remember, all things will work out; feel confident that God won't let you down. Has he ever jumped in the back seat of my limousine? Let the ride.

You came in like this with your faith leveled down.

But, turn it around and don't loose your faith, lift up high you know who you are!

Living your best life now and forever getting just what you ask and plan for!

What is your vision??

Why? Would you want that?

How? Will you go about achieving it?

When? Now is the time

God's greatest work is when you are going through your

trial!

Now let's plan…

What is your Goals

Start new Exposing Yourself too!

If you don't want to read, just look at the pictures. Your subconscious mind will put it all together for you.

All of this will help you build mental equipment of affluence, opulence, luxury and of course money.

New Prosperity!

Enjoy Life!

Worry Less!

Ask for the window of opportunity and guidance to take advantage and that your spirit remain in high so that you can receive all that's being sent to you! This is a well kept secret, but you get what you ask for.

It's the law of attraction and your belief and trust in the most high try it! The God in me is my unlimited overflowing source and supplier of all Goods!

Author's Contact Details

"You Get What You Ask For" Contact you author on:

Facebook

By Email: scjkeithshajackson@gmail.com

Radio – Television- Media

Request for speaking engagement

New Jersey

New York

Atlanta

Nationwide

For Television write
scjkeithshajackson@gmail.com

For Articles/ Pitch For Shows

Contact Author Shaaron Carswell Jackson

908-494-2721

Help to make this book a best seller by showing what you have read on twitter, facebook and purchasing a copy for a friend as a gift. There are many ways to celebrate this book.

Index

A

B

Blossom

____________**C**

Circumstance
Convenient
Commitment
Creating
Celebreties
Computer
Challenege
Conversation
Confident
Cultural
Concor
Criticize
Collectors
Cherish girl
Confidence.

____________**D**

Deliver
Dream opening
Driving
365 days
Depression
Date
Dedication
Dorothea
Difficulties
Destruction
Doubts

__________**E**

Escape from
Effects
Exercise
Earth
Everlast
Expec
tation
Faith
Evans
Entity
Existence
Eifel tower
Economic Crisis
Expensive
Experience

__________**F**

Father
Faith
Forgotten
Fabulous
Financial Help
Funeral Director
Fulfilled
Fulfillment
First Lady Michelle Obama __________**G**

Guidance

Growth
Goals – opening
God's Will
Great things opening
Glory
Graduation
Good living companion

____________**H**

Hawaii
Humble
Healing
Higher power
Heavenly father

____________**I**

Illness
Icon
Inventive
Inspiration
Imagine
Inaugurations

___________**J**

Jesus Name
Micheal Jackson
Journey

John
Jehov all

____
_K
Rob
ert
kiyo
saki
Kingdom
Kwanzah
Gayle king

____________**L**

Lifestyle
Life
Loyal
Like

____________**M**

Magical Faith
Ministered
Miracle
Manifestation
Manuscript
Mansion
Mathew

Mountains
Mother In Law
Mark
Mirror
Mark

____________**N**

No limit
Nitch
Naratives

___________**O**

Opportunity
Oprah Whitney
Outrageous
Dr Oz
Barack Obama

____________**P**

Procession
Powerful
Pistachio nut
Positive result
Persistent
Protect
Problem
Pray
Possible

Promise
Prosper
Pre conception
Paint a seed
Promoter
Preparing
Prescription
Purchasing
Production
Psalm
Paris
Persuasion
Progression
Persistence

____________**R**

Reaction
Reflect
Results
Religion
Recovery
Relationship
Record deal
Reservation
Relatives

___________**S**

Stretch
Shaken
Soul prosper
Solution

Self fulfillings
Spirit
Sources
Topic shaken
Substitute (opening pose)
Salmon
Seeker

___________**T**

Transform
Thought
Thinking
Trust
Trifold
Television host
Trust senosie

___________**U**

Ultimately
Uncertainly
Unjustified

____________**V**

Vital
Vision
Verbalizing beliefs
Value
Vision beard
Victoria

Crisis Scripture Guide

□ **Aging** Ps. 91:16 Prov. 9:11 Eccles. 12:1-8	□ **Debt** Ps. 37:21 Prov. 22:7 Rom. 13:8	□ **Freedom** Isa. 61:1 John 8:31-36 Rom. 6:22
□ **Anger** Prov. 15:1 Eph. 4:26-27 Col. 3:8	□ **Desires** Gal. 5:16 James 4:3 1 John 2:15-17	□ **Friendship** Prov. 17:17 Prov. 18:24 John 15:15-17
□ **Anxiety** Ps. 46:2-4 John 14:27 Phil. 4:6-8	□ **Dissatisfaction.** Phil. 4:11-13 1 Tim. 6:6-8) Heb. 13:5-6	□ **Future** Deut. 5:29 Jer. 29:11 Jer. 31:17
□ **Bitterness** Eph. 4:31 Heb. 12:15 James 3:14-15	□ **Doubt** Matt. 14:27-33 Matt. 21:21 James 1:6-8	□ **Gladness** Neh, 8:10-11 Ps. 118:24 Phil. 4:4
□ **Bondage** Rom, 6:18 John 8:32 2 Pet 2:19	□ **Encouragement** Ps. 23 John 16:33 James 1:2-4	□ **Gossip** Ps. 101:5 Prov, 18:8-9 Matt. 12:37
□ **Complaining** Phil. 2:14-16 James 5:9 1 Pet. 4:9	□ **Failure** Ps. 145:14-16 Prov. 24:16-18 Hab. 3:17-18	□ **Honesty** Ps. 32-2 Prov. 11:1-3 2 Cor. 4:2
□ **Courage** Josh. 1:9 Ps. 27:14 Hag, 2:4	□ **Fear** 2 Tim. 1:7 1 John 4:18 Rev. 1:17-18	□ **Hope** Rom. 5:2 1 Cor. 13:7 Col. 1:27
□ **Criticism** Luke 6:37 Rom. 8:1 Rom. 8:34	□ **Finances** Matt. 6:31-34 Mark 10:17:31 James 4:13-17	□ **Jealousy** Rom. 13:11-14 1 Cor. 3:3 1 Pet. 2:1-2

☐ **Death** Job 19:25-27 Isa, 25:8 1 Cor. 15:55	☐ **Forgiveness** Matt. 6:14-15 Luke 11:4 Eph.4:32	☐ **Joy** Ps. 16:11 Ps. 112:1 Rom. 7:22

☐ **Judgment** Matt. 7:2-5 Luke 6:37 Rev. 20:11-15	☐ **Perseverance** Matt, 10-22 Rom. 5:3-4 2 Pet. 1:5-7	☐ **Stress** Ps. 9:10 Ps. 73:261 Ps. 91:7-11
☐ **Prayer** Ps. 5:1-3 Ps. 138:3 Col. 4:21	☐ **Pride** Hosea 13:6 Matt. 18:2-4 2 Cor. 12:7-10	☐ **Success** Prov. 16:3 Mark 9:33-37 2 Cor. 3:5
☐ **Kindness** Eph. 4:32 1 Thess. 5:15 2 Tim. 2:24	☐ **Repentance** 2 Chron. 34:27 Ps. 7:12 Ps. 51:17	☐ **Suffering** Rom. 8:18-21 2 Cor. 4:8-9 1 Pet. 5:8-9
☐ **Laziness** Prov. 6:6 Prov. 10:4-5 Prov. 12:24	☐ **Rest** Exod. 20:8-10 Matt 11:28-29 Mark 6:31	☐ **Temptation** 1 Cor. 10:13 Gal. 6:1 James 1:2-4, 12-13
☐ **Lies** Exod. 20:16 Prov. 6:12-19 Prov. 19:5-9	☐ **Salvation** Ps. 27:1 Ps. 74:12 Isa. 25:9	☐ **Uncertainty** 1 Cor. 9:26 Heb. 10:23 James 1:6-8
☐ **Loneliness** Deut. 31:8 Ps. 23:4 John 14:18	☐ **Satan** Eph. 6:11-17 James 4:7 1 Pet. 5:8-9	☐ **Weakness** 2 Cor. 12:9 2 Cor. 13:4 Isa. 42:3
☐ **Marriage** Gen. 2:18 Matt, 19:3-8 Heb. 13:4	☐ **Sickness** Matt. 8:17 James 5:14 Rev. 21:3-4	☐ **Work** Hag.2:4 Matt. 6:24 Col. 3:23

□ **Obedience** 1 Sam. 15:22 Ps. 119:101 John 14:15	□ **Sinfulness** Ps. 25:6-8 Rom. 6:6-9 Eph.4:22-24	□ **Worldliness** Matt. 16:26 Mark 4:18-201 1 John 2:15-17
□ **Peace** John 14:27 Phil. 4:6-7 Col. 3:15	□ **Sorrow** Isa. 25:8 Matt. 5:4 Rom. 12:15	□ **Worship** Ps. 24:6 Ps. 150 Mark 7:7

About the Author

My name is Shaaron C Jackson, inventor Author, poet published in a lyrical Heritage Anthology of Poetry and SelfPublisher of Teenage Guide to Self-Development and Modeling Professional Model Commentator and Cosmetologist and Insurance Agent.

I have trained many in the modeling field and have had many Bubbling experiences that I share in this book; you get what you asked for; life is truly what people say it's amazing, and the things people and places can be turned around and seconds can be astonishing I started writing this book about my life and then directed by a higher power to direct my attention on faith and what it means to me and who leads me in the role to present you with my higher power of faith so make it a habit to be faithful person believing positively that God or your Superior of the highest will do things that will happen for you into you and the best for you learn to have a balance that's an important thing in life

Prescription for reading this book

"You Get What You Ask for",

Yes, there's a prescription for reading this book

You Get What You Ask For

I. Thought

II. Faith

III. Dream

IV. Believe

Side Effects

You won't lose your mind; you will live better; you will keep your Inner Spirit; you will be able to help others on their crisis; seek Higher Powers that you truly believe you will get what you asked for. You will be in control of your journey.

Reduce stress relievers as per Dr. OZ television; he said Exercise, Eat pistachio nuts and eat Salmon on a plate; these are some stress relieving things to eat and do.

Prayers for all Prayers for Prosperity and Guidance

Dear heavenly father, as I pray, allow this person reading this trajectory of it, allow for transformation for the better. Allow this person to understand where I was headed with this book and how I change due to higher power telling me, we are going to change the direction of this book! And now you will understand **You Get What You Ask for by putting faith to work!**

Made in the USA
Columbia, SC
23 June 2025